Eloise's Birthday Surprise

A VERY SPECIAL DAY

WRITTEN BY:
Jennifer Rose

ILLUSTRATIONS COLLABORATED WITH COPILOT
AND HAND EDITED WITH CANVA AND PHOTOPIA

PUBLISHED 2026

ILLUSTRATED BY:
Jessica Rose

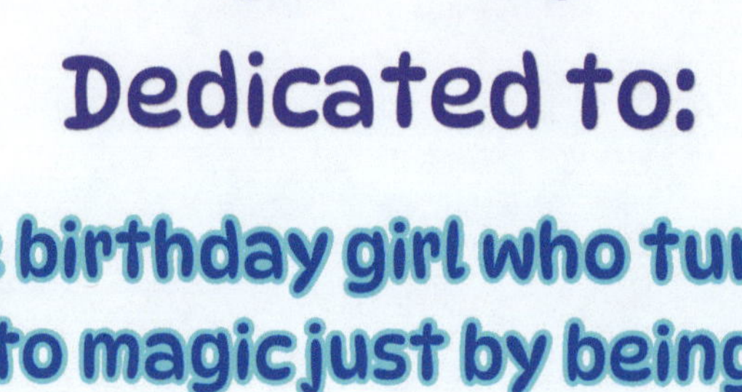

Dedicated to:

Eloise, the birthday girl who turns ordinary days into magic just by being herself.

For more books in this series, go to

http://thegigglenook.my.canva.site/giggleboxbooks

Giggle Box Books

This book belongs to...

____

(Your name)

An official member of the

Giggle Box Book Club

Eloise wakes up and cheers, “Today is my birthday, and I’m so excited!”

She runs into Mommy and Daddy's room and shouts, "It's time to wake up!" And her sisters join her.

Daddy yawns and says, “Happy Birthday...
...Let’s go make you birthday waffle!.”

Daddy makes a special waffle breakfast with fruit and warm chocolate. The kids' faces shine with sticky sweetness.

Daddy says,
“Let’s make
birthday crowns.”
He gives them
paper, glue, and
bright jewels.

Eloise is the birthday princess, smiling as Mommy snaps pictures of her and her sisters.

Mommy says, “Let’s take a walk
for your birthday.” They go to the
park with their dog.

The sisters bring their baby dolls to swing with them on the playground.

Daddy says, “Eloise, you can do the slide all by yourself now that you’re a big girl.”

After a long walk and fun at the park, the three sisters watch a show and then take a nap.

For lunch, they eat their favorite
pizza with a side of juicy watermelon.

After lunch Eloise says, "I wish my whole family was here for my birthday."
Daddy sighs, "Maybe they will call you."

They play a game so Eloise will smile, but she still misses the rest of her family.

Next, they go get birthday ice cream, but Eloise is still sad.

When they get home,
Mommy tells Eloise
she can go in first.

As the door swings open, everyone pops out and cheers, "Surprise! Happy Birthday!"

Her whole family comes together and sings "Happy Birthday!" to Eloise.

Grandma shouts, "Come look at all your presents!" Eloise's eyes grow wide and sparkle.

She wiggles and giggles with excitement as she unwraps each gift and is surprised.

Eloise lets her sisters look at her new dolls and dollhouse.

She gives everyone a big hug and says, "Thank you for my special day!"
HAPPY BIRTHDAY ELOISE!

Grandpa rolls out a shiny new bike he put together just for her.

The yard fills with giggles as she and her friends run around and play together.

Next, Mommy brings out a big birthday cake she made with candles.

Everyone sings Happy Birthday. Eloise makes a wish and blows out the candles.

Her Aunt asks, “What did you wish for?” Eloise says, “I wished I always get to see my family on all my birthdays.”

With a big hug, Mommy says, “We will always make sure you are with family on your birthdays because we love you!”

Blowing kisses, Eloise cheers, "The best thing about birthdays is time spent with family!"

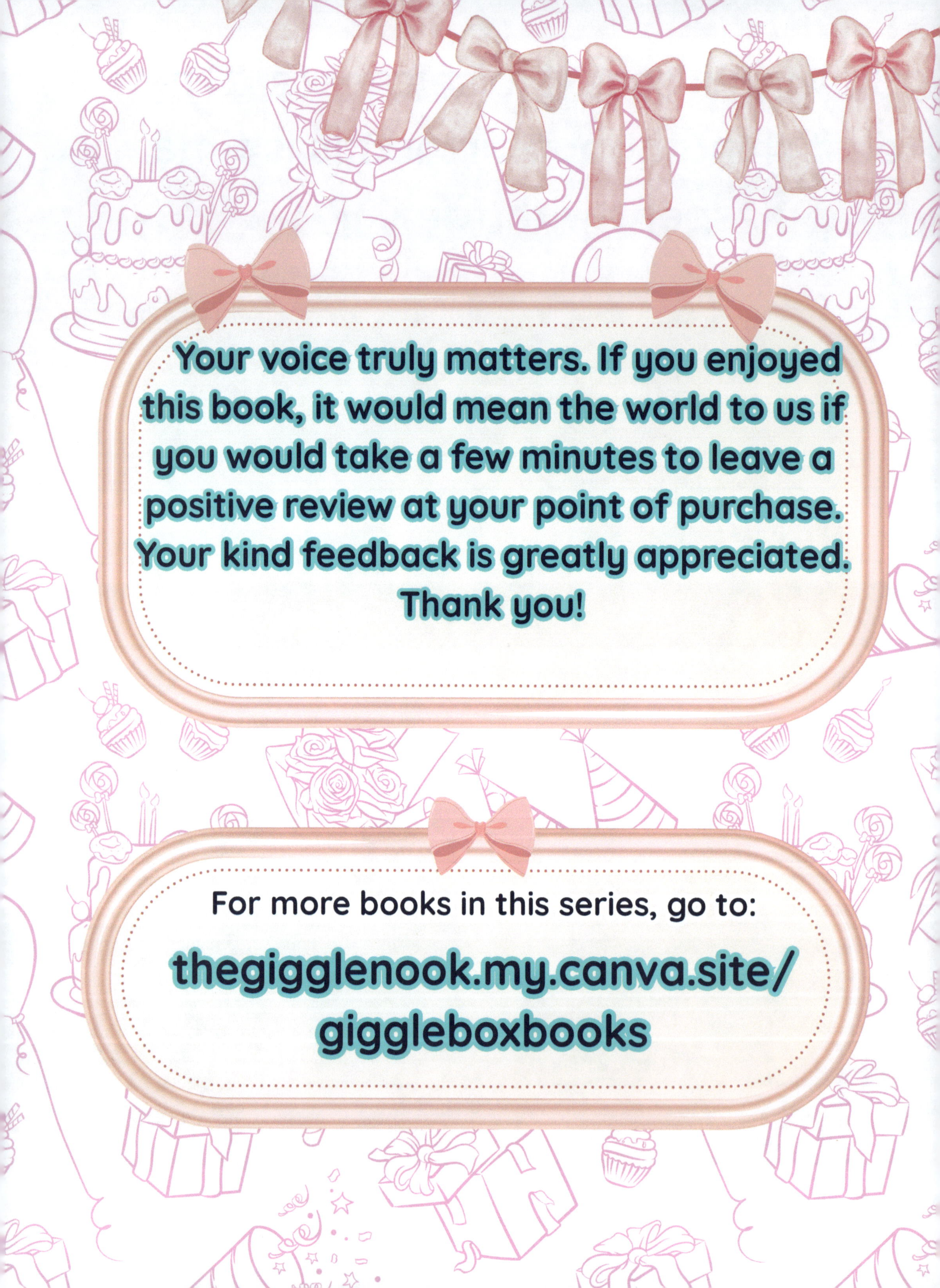
Your voice truly matters. If you enjoyed this book, it would mean the world to us if you would take a few minutes to leave a positive review at your point of purchase. Your kind feedback is greatly appreciated. Thank you!
For more books in this series, go to:
thegigglenook.my.canva.site/
giggleboxbooks

www.ingramcontent.com/pod-product-compliance
Lightning Source LLC
LaVergne TN
LVHW070204110826
845147LV00002B/498

* 9 7 8 1 9 6 9 1 7 3 2 6 4 *